Presented to

With love from

Date

GARY CHAPMAN

NORTHFIELD PUBLISHING
CHICAGO

Adapted from *The Five Love Languages*
Edited by: Tracey D. Lawrence

Cover and Interior Design: Smartt Guys design
Cover Photo: Michael Powers, Index Stock
Gary Chapman Photo: David Smith

ISBN: 1-881273-80-6
ISBN-13: 978-1-881273-80-6

We hope you enjoy this book from Northfield Publishing. Our goal is to provide high-quality, thought-provoking books and products that connect truth to your real needs and challenges. For more information on other books and products written and produced from a biblical perspective, go to www.moodypublishers.com or write to:

Northfield Publishing
215 West Locust Street
Chicago, IL 60610

5 7 9 10 8 6

Printed in Korea

CONTENTS

Chapter One

Why is it that so few couples seem to have found the secret to keeping love alive after the wedding? Why is it that a couple can attend a communication workshop, hear wonderful ideas on how to enhance communication, return home, and find themselves totally unable to implement the communication patterns demonstrated?

Finding the answer to these questions is the purpose of this book. It is not that the books and articles already published are not helpful. The problem is that we have overlooked one fundamental truth: People speak different love languages.

Most of us grow up learning the language

of our parents and siblings, which becomes our primary or native tongue. Later, we may learn additional languages but usually with much more effort. Language differences are part and parcel of human culture.

In the area of love, it is similar. Your emotional love language and the language of your spouse may be as different as Chinese from English. No matter how hard you try to express love in English, if your spouse understands only Chinese, you will never understand how to show love to each other. Being sincere is not enough. We must be willing to learn our spouse's primary love language if we are to be effective communicators of love.

My conclusion after thirty years of marriage counseling is that there are basically five emotional love languages—five ways that people speak and understand emotional love. However, there may be numerous dialects. The number of ways to express love within a love language is limited only by one's imagination. The important thing is to speak the love language of your spouse.

Once you identify and learn to speak your spouse's primary love language, I believe that you will have discovered the key to a long-lasting, loving marriage. Love need not evaporate after the wedding, but in order to keep it alive most of us will have to put forth the effort to learn a secondary love language.

At the heart of mankind's existence is the desire to be intimate and to be loved by another.

Marriage is designed to meet that need for intimacy and love. That is why the ancient biblical writings spoke of the husband and wife becoming "one flesh." That did not mean that individuals would lose their identity; it meant that they would enter into each other's lives in a deep and intimate way.

Again and again I have heard the words "Our love is gone, our relationship is dead. We used to feel close, but not now. We no longer enjoy being with each other. We don't meet each other's needs." Their stories bear testimony that adults as well as children have "love tanks."

I am convinced that keeping the emotional love tank full is as important to a marriage as maintaining the proper oil level is to an automobile. Running your marriage on an empty "love tank" may cost you even more than trying to drive your car without oil. Whatever the quality of your marriage now, it can always be better.

WARNING: Understanding the five love languages and learning to speak the primary love language of your spouse may radically affect his or her behavior. People behave differently when their emotional love tanks are full.

Before we examine the five love languages, however, we must address one other important but confusing phenomenon: the exhilarating experience of "falling in love."

At its peak, the "in love" experience is

euphoric. We are emotionally obsessed with each other. We go to sleep thinking of each other. When we wake up that person is the first thought on our minds. We long to be together.

The person who is "in love" has the illusion that his beloved is perfect.

We have been led to believe that if we are really in love, it will last forever. We will always have the wonderful feelings that we have at this moment. Nothing could ever come between us. Nothing will ever overcome our love for each other.

Eventually, however, we all descend from the clouds and plant our feet on earth again. Our eyes are opened, and we see the warts of the other person. We recognize that some of his/her personality traits are actually irritating. He has the capacity for hurt and anger, perhaps even harsh words and critical judgments. Those little traits that we overlooked when we were in love now become huge mountains.

Welcome to the real world of marriage, where hairs are always in the sink and little white spots cover the mirror, where arguments center on which way the toilet paper comes off and whether the lid should be up or down. In this world, a look can hurt and a word can crush. Intimate lovers can become enemies, and marriage a battlefield.

What happened to the "in love" experience? Alas, it was but an illusion by which we were tricked into signing our names on the dotted line, for better or for worse. Did we really have the "real" thing? I think so. The problem was faulty information.

The euphoria of the "in love" state gives us the illusion that we have an intimate relationship. We feel that we belong to each other. We believe we can conquer all problems.

Does that mean that, having been tricked into marriage by the illusion of being in love, we are now faced with just two options: (1) we are destined to a life of misery with our spouse, or (2) we must jump ship and try again?

There is a better alternative: We can recognize the in-love experience for what it was—a temporary emotional high—and now pursue "real love" with our spouse.

The emotional need for love must be met if we are to have emotional health. Married adults long to feel affection and love from their spouses. When your spouse's emotional love tank is full and he feels secure in your love, the whole world looks bright and your spouse will move out to reach his highest potential in life.

CHAPTER TWO

LOVE LANGUAGE #1

WORDS *of* *Affirmation*

One way to express love emotionally is to use words that build up. Solomon, author of some of the ancient Hebrew wisdom literature, wrote, "The tongue has the power of life and death."[1] Many couples have never learned the tremendous power of verbally affirming each other. Solomon further noted, "An anxious heart weighs a man down, but a kind word cheers him up."[2]

Verbal compliments, or words of appreciation, are powerful communicators of love. They are best expressed in simple, straightforward statements of affirmation, such as:

"You look sharp in that suit."

"Do you ever look nice in that dress! Wow!"

"You must be the best potato cook in the world. I love these potatoes."

"I really appreciate your washing the dishes tonight."

Encouraging Words

Giving verbal compliments is only one way to express words of affirmation to your spouse. Another dialect is encouraging words. The word encourage means "to inspire courage." All of us have areas in which we feel insecure. We lack courage, and that lack of courage often hinders us from accomplishing the positive things that we would like to do. The latent potential within your spouse in his or her areas of insecurity may await your encouraging words.

Most of us have more potential than we will ever develop. What holds us back is often courage. A loving spouse can supply that all-important catalyst. Of course, encouraging words may be difficult for you to speak. It may not be your primary love language. It may take great effort for you to learn this second language. That will be especially true if you have a pattern of using critical and condemning words, but I can assure you that it will be worth the effort.

Kind Words

Love is kind. If then we are to communicate love verbally, we must use kind words. That has to do with the way we speak. The same sentence can have two different meanings, depending on how you say it. The statement "I love you," when said with kindness and tenderness, can be a genuine expression of love. But what about the statement "I love you?" The question mark changes the whole meaning of those three words. Sometimes our words are saying one thing, but our tone of voice is saying another. We are sending double messages. Our spouse will usually interpret our message based on our tone of voice, not the words we use.

The manner in which we speak is exceedingly important. An ancient sage once said, "A soft answer turns away anger." When your spouse is angry and upset and lashing out words of heat, if you choose to be loving you will not reciprocate with additional heat but with a soft voice. If your motivation is different from what he is reading, you will be able to explain your motivation kindly. You will seek understanding and reconciliation, and not to prove your own perception as the only logical way to interpret what has happened. That is mature love—love to which we aspire if we seek a growing marriage.

Love doesn't keep a score of wrongs. Love doesn't bring up past failures. None of us is perfect. In marriage we do not always do the best or right thing. We have sometimes done and said hurtful things to our spouses. We cannot erase the past. We can only confess it and agree that it was wrong. We can ask for forgiveness and try to act differently in the future. If I choose justice and seek to pay my spouse back or make her pay for her wrongdoing, I am making myself the judge and her the felon. Intimacy becomes impossible. If, however, I choose to forgive, intimacy can be restored. Forgiveness is the way of love.

Humble Words

Love makes requests, not demands. When I demand things from my spouse, I become a parent and she the child. In marriage, however, we are equal, adult partners. We are not perfect to be sure, but we are adults and we are partners.

If we are to develop an intimate relationship, we need to know each other's desires. If we wish to love each other, we need to know what the other person wants.

The way we express those desires, however, is all-important. If they come across as demands, we have erased the possibility of intimacy and will drive our spouse away. If, however, we make known our needs and desires as requests, we are giving guidance, not ultimatums.

Various Dialects

Words of affirmation are one of the five basic love languages. Within that language, however, there are many dialects. We have discussed a few already, and there are many more. Entire volumes and numerous articles have been written on these dialects. All of the dialects have in common the use of words to affirm one's spouse. When you hear a lecture on love or you overhear a friend saying something positive about another person, write it down. In time, you will collect quite a list of words to use in communicating love to your spouse.

You may also want to try giving indirect words of affirmation, that is, saying positive things about your spouse when he or she is not present. Eventually, someone will tell your spouse, and you will get full credit for love. Tell your wife's mother how great your wife is. When her mother tells her what you said, your remarks will be amplified, and you will get even more credit. Also affirm your spouse in front of others when he or she is present. When you are given public honor for an accomplishment, be sure to share the credit with your spouse. You may also try your hand at writing words of affirmation. Written words have the benefit of being read over and over again.

If your spouse's love language is Words of Affirmation:

- Remind yourself: Words are important!

- Write a love letter

- Set a goal to compliment your spouse every day for one month.

CHAPTER THREE

LOVE LANGUAGE #2

Quality TIME

When I sit on the couch with my wife and give her twenty minutes of my undivided attention and she does the same for me, we are giving each other twenty minutes of life. We will never have those twenty minutes again; we are giving our lives to each other. It is a powerful emotional communicator of love.

Togetherness

A central aspect of quality time is togetherness. I do not mean proximity. Two people sitting in the same room are in close proximity, but they are not necessarily together. Togetherness has to do with focused attention. When a father is sitting on the floor, rolling a ball to his two-year-old, his attention is not focused on the ball but on his child. For that brief moment, however long it lasts, they are together. If, however, the father is talking on the phone while he rolls the ball, his attention is diluted.

Similarly, a husband and wife playing tennis together, if it is genuine quality time, will focus not on the game but on the fact that they are spending time together. What happens on the emotional level is what matters.

Quality Conversation

Like words of affirmation, the language of quality time also has many dialects. One of the most common dialects is that of quality conversation.

By quality conversation, I mean sympathetic dialogue where two individuals are sharing their experiences, thoughts, feelings, and desires in a friendly, uninterrupted context.

Quality conversation is quite different from the first love language. Words of affirmation focus on what we are saying, whereas quality conversation focuses on what we are hearing. If I am sharing my love for you by means of quality time and we are going to spend that time in conversation, it means I will focus on drawing you out, listening sympathetically to what you have to say.

A relationship calls for sympathetic listening with a view to understanding the other person's thoughts, feelings, and desires. Learning to listen may be as difficult as learning a foreign language, but learn we must, if we want to communicate love. Here is a summary of tips on how to listen:

1. Maintain eye contact when your spouse is talking.

2. Don't listen to your spouse and do something else at the same time.

3. Listen for feelings.

4. Observe body language.

5. Refuse to interrupt.

Learning to Talk

Quality conversation requires not only sympathetic listening but also self-revelation. When a wife says, "I wish my husband would talk. I never know what he's thinking or feeling," she is pleading for intimacy. In order for her to feel loved, he must learn to reveal himself. If her primary love language is quality time and her dialect is quality conversation, her emotional love tank will never be filled until he tells her his thoughts and feelings.

Not all of us are out of touch with our emotions, but when it comes to talking, all of us are affected by our personality. I have observed two basic personality types. The first I call the "Dead Sea." In the little nation of Israel, the Sea of Galilee flows south by way of the Jordan River into the Dead Sea. The Dead Sea goes nowhere. It receives but it does not give. This personality type receives many experiences, emotions, and thoughts throughout the day. They have a large reservoir where they store that information, and they are perfectly happy not to talk.

On the other extreme is the "Babbling Brook." For this personality, whatever enters into the eye gate or the ear gate comes out the mouth gate and there are seldom sixty seconds between the two. Whatever they see, whatever they hear, they tell. Many times a Dead Sea marries a Babbling Brook. That happens because when they are dating, it is a very attractive match.

But five years after marriage, the Babbling

Brook wakes up one morning and says, "We've been married five years, and I don't know him." The Dead Sea is saying, "I know her too well. I wish she would stop the flow and give me a break." The good news is that Dead Seas can learn to talk and Babbling Brooks can learn to listen. We are influenced by our personality but not controlled by it.

One way to learn new patterns is to establish a daily sharing time in which each of you will talk about three things that happened to you that day and how you feel about them. I call it the "Minimum Daily Requirement" for a healthy marriage. If you will start with the daily minimum, in a few weeks or months you may find quality conversation flowing more freely between you.

Quality Activities

Quality activities may include anything in which one or both of you have an interest. The emphasis is not on what you are doing but on why you are doing it. The purpose is to experience something together, to walk away from it feeling "He cares about me. He was willing to do something with me that I enjoy, and he did it with a positive attitude." That is love, and for some people it is love's loudest voice.

One of the by-products of quality activities is that they provide a memory bank from which to draw in the years ahead. Fortunate is the couple who remembers an early morning stroll along the coast, the spring they planted the flower garden, the time they got poison ivy chasing the rabbit through the woods. Those are memories of love, especially for the person whose primary love language is quality time.

If your spouse's love language is Quality Time:

- Take a walk together through the old neighborhood where one of you grew up. Ask questions about your spouse's childhood.

- Make a luncheon appointment with your spouse.

- Ask your spouse for a list of five activities that he would enjoy doing with you.

- Think of an activity your spouse enjoys, but which brings little pleasure to you.

Chapter Four

Love Language #3

Receiving Gifts

A gift is something you can hold in your hand and say, "Look, he was thinking of me," or "She remembered me." You must be thinking of someone to give him a gift. The gift itself is a symbol of that thought. It doesn't matter whether it costs money. What is important is that you thought of him. And it is not the thought implanted only in the mind that counts, but the thought expressed in actually securing the gift and giving it as the expression of love.

Gifts come in all sizes, colors, and shapes. Some are expensive, and others are free. To the individual whose primary love language is receiving gifts, the cost of the gift will matter little, unless it is greatly out of line with what you can afford. If a millionaire gives only one-dollar gifts regularly, the spouse may question whether that is an expression of love, but when family finances are limited, a one-dollar gift may speak a million dollars' worth of love.

Gifts and Money

If you are to become an effective gift giver, you may have to change your attitude about money. Each of us has an individualized perception of the purposes of money, and we have various emotions associated with spending it. Some of us have a spending orientation. We feel good about ourselves when we are spending money. Others have a saving and investing perspective. We feel good about ourselves when we are saving money and investing it wisely.

If you are a spender, you will have little difficulty purchasing gifts for your spouse; but if you are a saver, you will experience emotional resistance to the idea of spending money as an expression of love. If you discover that your spouse's primary love language is receiving gifts, then perhaps you will understand that purchasing gifts for him or her is the best investment you can make. You are investing in your relationship and filling your spouse's emotional love tank; and with a full love tank, he or she will likely reciprocate emotional love to you in a language you will understand.

The Gift of Self

There is an intangible gift that sometimes speaks more loudly than a gift that can be held in one's hand. I call it the gift of self or the gift of presence. Being there when your spouse needs you speaks loudly to the one whose primary love language is receiving gifts. Jan once said to me, "My husband, Don, loves softball more than he loves me."

"Why do you say that?" I inquired.

"On the day our baby was born, he played softball. I was lying in the hospital all afternoon while he played softball," she said.

"Was he there when the baby was born?"

"Oh, yes. He stayed long enough for the baby to be born, but ten minutes afterward, he left to play softball. I was devastated. It was such an important moment in our lives. I wanted us to share it together. I wanted him to be there with me. Don deserted me to play."

That husband may have sent her a dozen roses, but they would not have spoken as loudly as his presence in the hospital room beside her. The "baby" was now fifteen years old, and she was talking about the event with all the emotion as though it had happened yesterday. I probed further. "Have you based your conclusion that Don loves softball more than he loves you on this one experience?"

"Oh, no," she said. "On the day of my mother's funeral, he also played softball."

"Did he go to the funeral?"

"Oh, yes. He went to the funeral, but as soon as it was over, he left to play softball. I couldn't believe it. My brothers and sisters came to the house with me, but my husband was playing softball."

Later, I asked Don about those two events. He knew exactly what I was talking about. "I knew she would bring that up," he said. "I was there through all the labor and when the baby was born. I took pictures; I was so happy. I couldn't wait to tell the guys on the team, but my bubble was burst when I got back to the hospital that evening. She was furious with me. I couldn't believe what she was saying. I thought she would be proud of me for telling the team.

"And when her mother died? She probably

did not tell you that I took off work a week before she died and spent the whole week at the hospital and at her mother's house doing repairs and helping out. After she died and the funeral was over, I felt I had done all I could do. I needed a breather. I like to play softball, and I knew that would help me relax and relieve some of the stress I'd been under. I thought she would want me to take a break.

"I had done what I thought was important to her, but it wasn't enough. She has never let me forget those two days. She says that I love softball more than I love her. That's ridiculous."

He was a sincere husband who failed to understand the tremendous power of presence. His being there for his wife was more important than anything else in her mind. Physical presence in the time of crisis is the most powerful gift you can give if your spouse's primary love language is receiving gifts.

If the physical presence of your spouse is important to you, I urge you to verbalize that to your spouse. Don't expect him to read your mind. If, on the other hand, your spouse says to you, "I really want you to be there with me tonight, tomorrow, this afternoon," take his request seriously.

Almost everything ever written on the subject of love indicates that at the heart of love is the spirit of giving. All five love languages challenge us to give to our spouse, but for some, receiving gifts, visible symbols of love, speaks the loudest.

If your spouse's love language is Receiving Gifts:

- Try a parade of gifts: Leave a box of candy for your spouse in the morning (yogurt candy if health is an issue); have flowers delivered in the afternoon (unless your spouse is allergic to flowers); give him a shirt in the evening.

- Make a gift for your spouse.

- Give your spouse a gift every day for one week.

CHAPTER FIVE

LOVE LANGUAGE #4

ACTS *of* *Service*

Jesus Christ gave a simple but profound illustration of expressing love by an act of service when He washed the feet of His disciples. In a culture where people wore sandals and walked on dirt streets, it was customary for the servant of the household to wash the feet of guests as they arrived. Jesus, who had instructed His disciples to love one another, gave them an example of how to express that love when He took a basin and a towel and proceeded to wash their feet.[1] After that simple expression of love, He encouraged His disciples to follow His example.

Earlier in His life, Jesus had indicated that in His kingdom those who would be great would be servants. In most societies, those who are great lord it over those who are small, but Jesus Christ said that those who are great would serve others. The apostle Paul summarized that philosophy when he said, "Serve one another in love."[2]

Doormat or Lover?

"I have served him for twenty years. I have waited on him hand and foot. I have been his doormat while he ignored me, mistreated me, and humiliated me in front of my friends and family. I don't hate him. I wish him no ill, but I resent him, and I no longer wish to live with him." That wife has performed acts of service for twenty years, but they have not been expressions of love. They were done out of fear, guilt, and resentment.

A doormat is an inanimate object. You can wipe your feet on it, step on it, kick it around, or whatever you like. It has no will of its own. It can be your servant but not your lover. When we treat our spouses as objects, we preclude the possibility of love. Manipulation by guilt ("If you were a good spouse, you would do this for me") is not the language of love. Coercion by fear ("You will do this or you will be sorry") is alien to love. No person should ever be a doormat. Love says, "I love you too much to let you treat me this way. It is not good for you or me."

Overcoming Stereotypes

Learning the love language of acts of service will require some of us to reexamine our stereotypes of the roles of husbands and wives. Mark was doing what most of us do naturally. He was following the role model of his father and mother, but he wasn't even doing that well. His father washed the car and mowed the grass. Mark did not, but that was the mental image he had of what a husband should do. He definitely did not picture himself vacuuming floors and changing the baby's diapers. To his credit, he was willing to break from his stereotype when he realized how important it was to Mary. That is necessary for all of us if our spouse's primary love language asks something of us that seems inappropriate to our role.

Due to the sociological changes of the past thirty years, there is no longer a common stereotype of the male and female role in American society. Yet that does not mean that all stereotypes have been removed. It means rather that the number of stereotypes has been multiplied. With the pervasiveness of television and the proliferation of single-parent families, however, role models are often influenced by forces outside the home. Whatever your perceptions, chances are your spouse perceives marital roles somewhat differently than you do. A willingness to examine and change stereotypes is necessary in order to express love more effectively.

Recently a wife said to me, "Dr. Chapman, I am going to send all of my friends to your seminar."

"And why would you do that?" I inquired.

"Because it has radically changed our marriage," she said. "Before the seminar, Bob never helped me with anything. We both started our careers right after college, but it was always my role to do everything at the house. It was as if it never crossed his mind to help me with anything. After the seminar, he started asking me, 'What can I do to help you this evening?' It was amazing. At first, I couldn't believe it was real, but it has persisted for three years now.

"I'll have to admit, there were some trying and humorous times in those early weeks because he didn't know how to do anything. The first time he did the laundry, he used undiluted bleach instead of regular detergent. Our blue towels came out with white polka dots. . . . But he was loving me in my language, and my tank was filling up. . . . Believe me, I have learned his language, and I keep his tank full."

Is it really that simple?

Simple? Yes. Easy? No. Bob had to work hard at tearing down the stereotype with which he had lived for thirty-five years. It didn't come easily, but he would tell you that learning the primary love language of your spouse and choosing to speak it makes a tremendous difference in the emotional climate of a marriage.

If your spouse's love language is Acts of Service:

- Make a list of all the requests your spouse has made of you over the past few weeks. Select one of these each week and do it as an expression of love.

- Give your spouse a love note accompanied by the act of service every three days for a month.

- Get the children to help you with some act of service for him or her.

CHAPTER SIX

LOVE LANGUAGE #5

PHYSICAL *Touch*

Physical touch is also a powerful vehicle for communicating marital love. Holding hands, kissing, embracing, and sexual intercourse are all ways of communicating emotional love to one's spouse. For some individuals, physical touch is their primary love language. Without it, they feel unloved. With it, their emotional tank is filled, and they feel secure in the love of their spouse.

Physical touch can make or break a relationship. It can communicate hate or love. To the person whose primary love language is physical touch, the message will be far louder than the words "I hate you" or "I love you." A slap in the face is detrimental to any child, but it is devastating to a child whose primary love language is touch. A tender hug communicates love to any child, but it shouts love to the child whose primary love language is physical touch. The same is true of adults.

In marriage, the touch of love may take many forms. Since touch receptors are located throughout the body, lovingly touching your spouse almost anywhere can be an expression of love. That does not mean that all touches are created equal. Some will bring more pleasure to your spouse than others. Your best instructor is your spouse, of course. After all, she is the one you are seeking to love. She knows best what she perceives as a loving touch. Don't insist on touching her in your way and in your time. Learn to speak her love dialect. Don't make the mistake of believing that the touch that brings pleasure to you will also bring pleasure to her.

Love touches may be explicit and demand your full attention such as in a back rub or sexual foreplay, culminating in intercourse. On the other hand, love touches may be implicit and require only a moment, such as putting your hand on his shoulder as you pour a cup of coffee or rubbing your body against him as you pass in the kitchen. Explicit love touches obviously take more time, not only in actual touching but in developing your understanding of how to communicate love to your spouse this way. If a back massage communicates love loudly to your spouse, then the time, money, and energy you spend in learning to be a good masseur or masseuse will be well invested. If sexual intercourse is your mate's primary dialect, reading about and discussing the art of sexual lovemaking will enhance your expression of love.

Implicit love touches require little time but much thought, especially if physical touch is not your primary love language and if you did not grow up in a "touching family." Sitting close to each other on the couch as you watch your favorite television program requires no additional time but may communicate your love loudly. Touching your spouse as you walk through the room where he is sitting takes only a moment. Touching each other when you leave the house and again when you return may involve only a brief kiss or hug but will speak volumes to your spouse.

The Body Is for Touching

Whatever there is of me resides in my body. To touch my body is to touch me. To withdraw from my body is to distance yourself from me emotionally. In our society shaking hands is a way of communicating openness and social closeness to another individual. When on rare occasions one man refuses to shake hands with another, it communicates a message that things are not right in their relationship.

Crisis and Physical Touch

Almost instinctively in a time of crisis, we hug one another. Why? Because physical touch is a powerful communicator of love. In a time of crisis, more than anything, we need to feel loved. We cannot always change events, but we can survive if we feel loved.

All marriages will experience crises. The death of parents is inevitable. Automobile accidents cripple and kill thousands each year. Disease is no respecter of persons. Disappointments are a part of life. The most important thing you can do for your mate in a time of crisis is to love him or her. If your spouse's primary love language is physical touch, nothing is more important than holding her as she cries. Your words may mean little, but your physical touch will communicate that you care. Crises provide a unique opportunity for expressing love. Your tender touches will be remembered long after the crisis has passed. Your failure to touch may never be forgotten.

If your spouse's love language is Physical Touch:

- As you walk from the car to the shopping mall, reach out and hold your spouse's hand.

- When your spouse arrives at home, meet him or her one step earlier than usual and give your mate a big hug.

- Initiate sex by giving your spouse a foot massage.

Chapter Seven

Discovering *Love* that Lasts

Discovering the primary love language of your spouse is essential if you are to keep his/her emotional love tank full. But first, let's make sure you know your own love language. Having heard the five emotional love languages,

Words of Affirmation
Quality Time
Receiving Gifts
Acts of Service
Physical Touch

some individuals will know instantaneously their own primary love language and that of their spouse. For others, it will not be that easy.

What is your primary love language? What makes you feel most loved by your spouse? What do you desire above all else?

I have suggested three ways to discover your own primary love language.

1. *What does your spouse do or fail to do that hurts you most deeply? The opposite of what hurts you most is probably your love language.*

2. *What have you most often requested of your spouse? The thing you have most often requested is likely the thing that would make you feel most loved.*

3. *In what way do you regularly express love to your*

spouse? Your method of expressing love may be an indication that that would also make you feel loved.

Love Is a Choice

How can we speak each other's love language when we are full of hurt, anger, and resentment over past failures? The answer to that question lies in the essential nature of our humanity. We are creatures of choice. That means that we have the capacity to make poor choices, which all of us have done. We have spoken critical words, and we have done hurtful things. We are not proud of those choices, although they may have seemed justified at the moment. Poor choices in the past don't mean that we must make them in the future. Instead we can say, "I'm sorry. I know I have hurt you, but I would like to make the future different. I would like to love you in your language. I would like to meet your needs." I have seen marriages rescued from the brink of divorce when couples make the choice to love.

Love doesn't erase the past, but it makes the future different. When we choose active expressions of love in the primary love language of our spouse, we create an emotional climate where we can deal with our past conflicts and failures.

Meeting my wife's need for love is a choice I make each day. If I know her primary love language and choose to speak it, her deepest emotional need will be met and she will feel secure in my love. If she does the same for me, my emotional needs are met and both of us live with a full tank. In a state of emotional contentment, both of us will give our creative energies to many wholesome projects outside the marriage while we continue to keep our marriage exciting and growing.

Most of us do many things each day that do not come "naturally" for us. For some of us, that is getting out of bed in the morning. We go against our feelings and get out of bed. Why? Because we believe there is something worthwhile to do that day. And normally, before the day is over, we feel good about having gotten up. Our actions preceded our emotions.

The same is true with love. We discover the primary love language of our spouse, and we choose to speak it whether or not it is natural for us. We are not claiming to have warm, excited feelings. We are simply choosing to do it for his or her benefit. We want to meet our spouse's emotional need, and we reach out to speak his love language. In so doing, his emotional love tank is filled and chances are he will reciprocate and speak our language. When he does, our emotions return, and our love tank begins to fill.

Love is a choice. And either partner can start the process today.

Loves Makes a Difference

Love is not our only emotional need. Psychologists have observed that among our basic needs are the need for security, self-worth, and significance. Love, however, interfaces with all of those.

If I feel loved by my spouse, I can relax, knowing that my lover will do me no ill. I feel secure in his/her presence. I may face many uncertainties in my vocation. I may have enemies in other areas of my life, but with my spouse I feel secure.

My sense of self-worth is fed by the fact that my spouse loves me. After all, if he/she loves me, I must be worth loving. My parents may have given me negative or mixed messages about my worth, but my spouse knows me as an adult and loves me. Her love builds my self-esteem.

The need for significance is the emotional force behind much of our behavior. Life is driven by the desire for success. We want our lives to count for something. We have our own idea of what it means to be significant, and we work hard to reach our goals. Feeling loved by a spouse enhances our sense of significance. We reason, If someone loves me, I must have significance.

In the context of marriage, if we do not feel loved, our differences are magnified. We come to view each other as a threat to our happiness. We fight for self-worth and significance, and marriage becomes a battlefield rather than a haven.

Love is not the answer to everything, but it creates a climate of security in which we can seek answers to those things that bother us. In the security of love, a couple can discuss differences without condemnation. Conflicts can be resolved.

Two people who are different can learn to live together in harmony. We discover how to bring out the best in each other. Those are the rewards of love.

Can emotional love be reborn in a marriage? You bet. The key is to learn the primary love language of your spouse and choose to speak it.

NOTES

Chapter 2

1. Proverbs 18:21.
2. Proverbs 12:25.

Chapter 5

1. John 13:3–17.
2. Galatians 5:13.

The Relationship-Enhancing Phenomenon that Started It All!

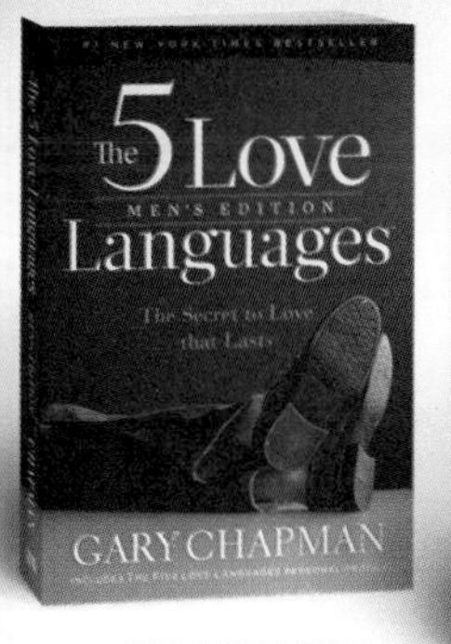

978-0-8024-7316-5

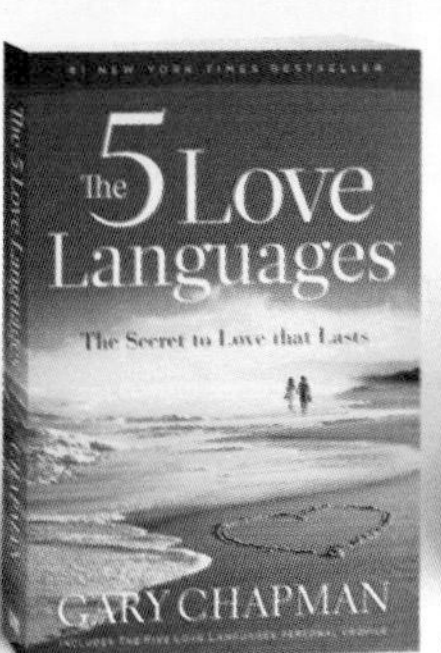

978-0-8024-7315-8

978-0-8024-7362-2

The 5 Love Languages®

In the full-length edition of his #1 *New York Times* bestseller Dr. Gary Chapman uses real-life examples from over 40 years of marriage counseling to illustrate the five distinct languages people use to express love. *The 5 Love Languages*® can breathe new life into your relationships. Available in three editions: standard, Men's Edition, and Gift Edition.

Visit 5LoveLanguages.com

also available as ebooks

Your Wedding Day is Just the Beginning

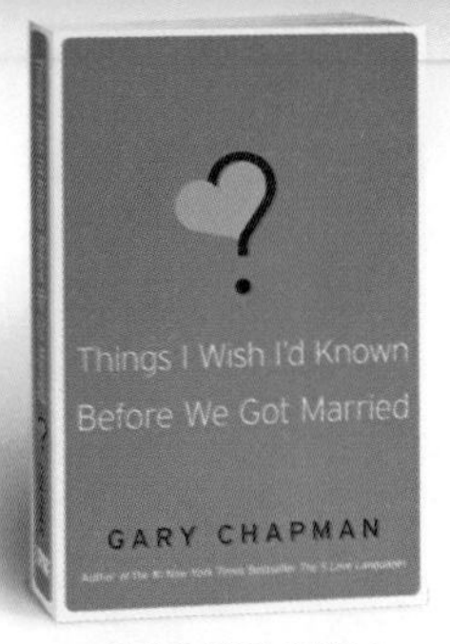

978-0-8024-8183-2

Things I Wish I'd Known Before We Got Married

A practical, must-read book for ALL dating, engaged, and recently married couples.

- Learning exercises
- Helpful resources
- "Talking It Over" sections
- Thought-provoking appendix

Visit ThingsIWishBook.com

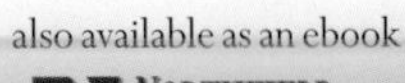